Don't Go

Thrifting

Without Me

**A Mini Guide to Maximize the
Benefits of Thrifting**

Adrienne S. Young

Copyright

DEDICATION

I dedicate this book to my late grandmother, Della Louise Manning, who passed away when my mother was only 20 years old. My mother shared with me when she died, there were beautiful slips in her drawer, unworn with tags still on them. When people marvel at me wearing sequin tops with heels at the grocery store, I say thank you knowing my "why" is because I don't want to die having things unworn in my closet waiting for a special occasion. When I thrift and walk past beautiful slips with tags still on them, I touch them and think of her.

ACKNOWLEDGMENTS

I would not be able to pen one word in this book without my God, the only true and living God. He gave me this passion, and although I thought it was the be all plan for my life (just google my old blogs), He had a better plan in mind. Thank you, Father, for allowing me to partner with you to write this book and allowing me thrift again. I promise to not overdo it this time.

My husband is the most amazing man ever. He has been my number one supporter in every venture in life and every time he goes thrifting with me, he always brings me the most hideous thing to make me laugh. I love you so much, Babe. Thank you for allowing me to shop for hours, to buy your thrift clothes, and for pushing me to greatness.

To my boys who never felt ashamed to wear thrifted items and for celebrating with me when I found things for them… Thank you for allowing Mom to host swap parties on Sundays and you both leaving the house so that all my friends and I would have space. You boys are the best!

To my Mom who is my thrift partner and allows me to use her senior discount on Tuesdays (don't judge me)… I appreciate your support in all that I do and for always buying me great thrifted pieces that scream my name!

To Melissa J. Nixon who said a prayer for writers during her 21 days of prayer for entrepreneurs… During that prayer, fire hit my fingers, and I completed this book in two weeks. You, my sister, are an activator, and I am grateful to call you my friend and business bestie.

To my friend, Roshanda "The RoSho" Pratt, thank you for allowing me to take you thrifting for the very first time and for writing this amazing foreword! You have inspired me beyond words, and I am grateful to have you in my life.

To my brother, Rickie Sarratt, who I called and asked to do this book cover without giving him a vision for it… Brother, you captured it all!! I LOVE you so much. Over and an over again you come through for me.

To Otescia Johnson, my editor, PR, and everything else... Thank you for responding to my 11 pm email to write this book. Your first yes to me opened this door. I look forward to writing many more books together.

To each of my thrift sisters who said YES to me interviewing them for this book, THANK YOU. You brought more value to the readers, and for those who I chatted with on the phone, we had the best time! I pray I get to go thrifting with each of you.

My Thrift Scripture

"So here's what I want you to do, God helping you: Take your everyday, ordinary life—your sleeping, eating, going-to-work, and walking-around life—and place it before God as an offering. Embracing what God does for you is the best thing you can do for him. Don't become so well-adjusted to your culture that you fit into it without even thinking. Instead, fix your attention on God. You'll be changed from the inside out. Readily recognize what he wants from you, and quickly respond to it. Unlike the culture around you, always dragging you down to its level of immaturity, God brings the best out of you, develops well-formed maturity in you." Romans 12:1-2 MSG

Don't Go *Thrifting* Without Me!
Foreword

Fashion Icon Coco Chanel said, "If a woman is poorly dressed, you notice her dress, and if she's impeccably dressed, you notice the woman."

I am elated my stylish friend, Adrienne Young, decided to empower and inspire women everywhere to get noticed without going to the poor house to do it. I recently had the opportunity of finally going thrifting with her for the first time. Ladies and gentlemen, it was an experience I won't forget! Maybe you are like me and always wanted to go thrifting, but the thought seems overwhelming, or maybe you have gone thrifting before but need a strategy to get the most out of your experience. Whatever the reason, you don't want to go thrifting without Adrienne!

My thrift experience was exhilarating. My first haul yielded a pair of Guess heels, a Versona Kimono, leopard print skirt, a Michael Kors bag, and a few items for my daughters. I don't think I even spent 50 bucks! I was floored! Adrienne taught me how to:
- Dress for the shopping experience
- Strategy to maximize our time in the store
- How to clean my items afterwards

Adrienne S. Young

As a busy wife, mom, storyteller and live video strategist, having direction takes away the guess work and one thing off my growing checklist. Before you plan your next shopping experience either solo or with a group of friends, take this thrifting guide and your new best friend, Adrienne Young with you. Do you and your wallet a favor and go thrifting with Adrienne. *"Don't Go Thrifting Without Me"* is your step-by-step style guide to looking impeccable and being noticed on a dime.

To see one of our many shopping experiences, check out my YouTube page:
https://www.youtube.com/channel/UCUaF2GsbwV9gpiVa6CpebAw

You can also catch Adrienne and I in action here:
https://youtu.be/5KalS8HjurA

Happy Thrifting!

-Roshanda *"The Rosho"* Pratt

Don't Go *Thrifting* Without Me!

My Thrift Prayer

Father, thank you for allowing me the income to thrift and for those who donate items. My prayer is when I go into this store, allow me to see what you have for me. Whatever is in on my Wishlist, should it be here, let me see it and let it be without malfunctions. If someone is holding an item in their hand, and I know it is for me, allow me to patiently wait for them to put it back so that I can get it (lol) in Jesus name, AMEN!

Book Cover Attire

Yes, everything you see in the cover photo is thrifted!

- Sequin blouse: $2 from Pawsbility Thrift Shop
- Leather Pants: $12 from the annual Green Jeans Consignment Sale
- Steve Madden Red Pumps: $4.99 from Goodwill
- Jessica Simpson Black Clutch: $3.99 from Goodwill
- Dangle earrings: $2.99 from Goodwill

Don't Go *Thrifting* Without Me!

Introduction

WHY Thrift Shop?

The smell is musty. The shopping cart wheels squeak. There are hangers on the floor. No one greets me when I walk in, but all that doesn't matter when I spot the leather pants I saw in the mall for $99 for $4.99! I have entered the world of thrifting, and I know this shopping trip is going to be epic.

I remember the day I fell in love with thrifting. I had just finished watching my favorite TV show, What Not to Wear, and my in-laws blessed me with $100 for Christmas. I could not afford and $80 blouse or $150 slacks like those on the show. I knew I needed a more professional look for my career as a school counselor, and I knew thrifting was the solution. I made a list of all the staples Stacy said I needed, walked into the local Goodwill in Charleston, SC and bought every single piece, with change to spare. The canary yellow cashmere sweater I scored made me feel like a hundred bucks when I wore it. From that day forward, I knew thrift shopping was for me.

I often ask myself if I became a millionaire, would I still thrift? I'm 99.99% sure I would! The thrill of the hunt alone is worth it. I get giddy when I walk in a store, inhale the stale smell (of some stores), grab a cart, and stroll down the aisles knowing I will leave with a great deal. Although this book is mostly about thrifting clothing, I have found just as great of deals for home decor. From lamps to bookshelves, and mirrors, my home is just as thrifty as my closet!

You may be asking, why would you thrift shop when you can find an item on clearance for probably the same amount, if not lower, and you don't have to worry about the smell, or inspecting for possible malfunctions? I'll admit there are times when I don't want the hassle and order items online or head to a department store; however, if you are on a budget (especially college students and young adults entering the workforce), enjoy finding treasures, and want to score some staple or unique pieces, try thrifting! Maybe you need a new wardrobe because of weight loss, a new career, or you want a few go-to pieces in your closet for special occasions. Regardless, of your reason, it is the goal of this book to teach you how to thrift so that you can dress your best for less!

Whether you have the paperback or eBook, keep it close by while thrifting to serve as a guide. Highlight and bookmark sections you don't want to forget, and should you not need the guide anymore, bless someone with your copy! Make it more memorable by taking a first timer thrifting and giving him or her this book as a gift!

I will caution you: your first-time thrifting may be overwhelming so be sure to take someone with you (I talk more about the thrifting buddy later in the book). I have partnered with amazing thrifters who I admire to give you insight, secrets, and confidence in your journey. Their stories will motivate you and when you follow them on social media, you will receive inspiration. When you go thrifting, have fun! Laugh at the items from the twin sisters "Poly and Esther," reminisce on the shoulder pads worn in the 80s at the school dances and jump for joy when you score a brand new dress for $1! It is time to go, and this time… don't go thrifting without me!

Thrifting for Clothes and Accessories

Have a Thrifting Plan.

Just like when we go to the grocery store hungry without a list and buy everything, such is the fate of those who go thrifting without a list and buy everything. It does not matter it was only $0.50 if you already have four red blouses. Speaking of four blouses, I strongly suggest you purge your closet once a quarter or at least twice a year (in the fall and spring) so that you can make room for your new goodies. Donate your items or have a swap party (see the end of the book as to how) to bless others. Try not to have so many pieces in your closet and drawers that you cannot see the leather peplum top and miss wearing it all season long. Your brain loves a plan, and when you make a list of the items you want to find while thrifting, your mind is ready to hunt for it and more than likely, it will see it.

In your plan, make sure you have a budget. To stick with it, use cash or maybe a prepaid card with the amount allotted. Does this mean you have to pass on the sequin top not on your list? Absolutely not! It just says you are intentional in your thrift shopping, and you have self-discipline. If you genuinely want an item, ask the store associate if he or she can hold it for you until tomorrow. If you love the find, you will

Don't Go *Thrifting* Without Me!

come back and get it and bring it to its new home.
You still have a plan, and this plan will pay off!

The Ideal Time to Thrift

It's Monday morning, and all weekend long people have dropped their unwanted items off to your local thrift store. You wake up with anticipation of what you will find and take out your list of what you want to score. When you arrive, the associates are stocking the shelves and bringing out racks of new clothes, and you are ready for the hunt!

Many thrift stores offer discount days and times for additional savings. For instance, Upstate, South Carolina Goodwill stores have a color tag of the week that is 50% off the first couple of days of the week, and then those items tagged with that color are $1 the remaining days. On the weekend, the price goes down to .50! If you have time, scope out what they have on Monday, and then go back on Thursday to grab your bargains. Shopping early in the morning is best because not as many people are there and the dressing rooms, for those who have them, are readily available.

How to Dress to Thrift

You may be thinking, "Wait, you have to dress a certain way to go thrift shopping?" Technically, you do not, but if you want to save time, you should have what fellow thrifter Keren Charles of Thrifting Atlanta calls a "thrifting uniform." If you are not comfortable getting undressed to try on items, if you are stretched for time and don't have time to wait for the dressing room, or if there are not dressing rooms in a store, here's what you can wear:

- **Option 1 (pictured):**
    - fitted camisole or tee
    - leggings or jeggings
    - duster or a blazer
    - shoes of your choice*
- **Option 2:**
    - fitted camisole or tee
    - leggings or jeggings
    - trench coat or kimono
    - shoes of your choice*

I had one fellow thrifter recommend a catsuit, but I use the bathroom way too much to unzip all of that. Each option allows you to slip items on and off easily without exposing yourself to others.

What Not to Wear

Omit big jewelry such as hoop earrings as it makes slipping items on and off more difficult. Although my stylist prefers necklaces over necks, I do not wear one for the same reason as hoops unless I can take it off easily. Also, you may want to steer away from makeup to avoid staining any clothing.

I prefer to thrift in a comfortable shoe, especially if I plan to go to a few stores in one trip. However, take a nude heel with you so that when you try on slacks or dresses, you can get a sense of a completed look to make a final decision. #styletipsbySoancera

Don't Go *Thrifting* Without Me!

Thrifting Interview
Keren Charles | Thrifting Atlanta

Thrift • Fashion • Stylist

"So, it became a lifestyle for me."

What or who led you to join the world of thrifting?

My inspiration started when I was in high school. My mom, who always thrifted, would bring me these beautiful outfits, but I would never want to be seen in the store. I didn't want to thrift because back then, when I was in high school in the early nineties, it was really like a taboo to be seen in there. People always thought that you were poor, you were homeless, and that you couldn't afford clothes. I didn't want my friends to see me in there, but when I started working at my first job, I worked at Popeye's, and we had to buy black pants to wear with our shirts. And my mom was like, "Why are you going to the mall to buy something that is going to get dirty? Why don't you just go to the thrift store?" I listened to her and because of that day when I went in, and I saw all these amazing pieces of clothes and shoes, I fell in love.

Advice for first time thrifter:

My first timers, I always tell them to not be overwhelmed because, thrifting is not like when you go in a regular department store where you have mannequins, and you can say I need this in a medium. When you thrift, make sure it's something that you love even if it's fifty cents, $1, or $10. Shop with an experienced thrifter and allow them to walk you through garments, and also dress you. Eventually you'll just start to feel like, okay... I think I can do this on my own.

Best thrifted item:

My most recent purchase that was at Goodwill is my best thrifted item. I always walked by the purses and then I go to the dresses. I went through the area, walking by the purses, and I see a Louis Vuitton. I did a double take because I'm like, wait, is this real? So, because I love Louis Vuitton, (I have one that was gifted to me) I know what to look for. I looked inside for the serial number, the monogram, the lining and I was like, oh my God. Jesus. Thank you! It was $3.99!!

What will you never thrift?

I will not thrift underwear or bras. But if it's vintage, I will. I love slips. I love the lace. I'm old school, so I like a slip every now and then.

What do you always thrift?

I love dresses because they make you feel so girly. It's easy to throw on. I'm obsessed with sequins so if I see something sparkling, I'm going to that section!

How has your thrifting enhanced someone else's life?

Well, there was a lady, in the group I used to thrift with. She said that she did not thrift. She stated, "I love home decor and beautiful pillows, but I won't wear other people's clothes." I was like, "Ma'am, if you think about it, if you stopped at Marshalls for clothes and then you decide to try them on, how many people before you tried on that same garment? Someone may have come from the gym, went shopping, and they're all sweaty and stinky and they've tried on the same outfit. She didn't have anything to say by the end of that. Now, she is the one racking up all the time, and she posts all these outfits in the group. So, we were able to change her perspective about wearing other people's clothing for lack of knowledge. Fashion is creating community and basically helping people. It is also creating a space where they feel welcome.

Share a thrifting secret.

Wear a thrifting uniform, stand by the mirror, and try on the clothes. That way you are not limited by how many pieces you can take into the dressing room.

Favorite thrift stores and why:

In Atlanta, one of my favorite consignment stores is Alexis Consignment. That's where I go for designer bags and shoes. Chanel, Louis Vuitton and Gucci.

HOW CAN WE CONNECT WITH YOU?

Two Stylish Kays

Website- www.twostylishkays.com
Facebook- www.facebook.com/twostylishkays
Twitter- www.twitter.com/twostylishkays
Instagram- www.instagram.com/twostylishkays
Facebook Group- www.facebook.com/groups/thriftingatlanta

The Ideal Way to Thrift

Your plan has been laid out, you wake up to get dressed, and you grab your normal shoulder bag. BIG mistake! Unless you enjoy being bumped by your bag or pushing it out the way several times while getting items, leave the handbag at home. Instead, grab a wristlet, a crossbody bag, or simply have your card, id and/or cash in your pocket. You need your arms to be free!

Speaking of free, grab a shopping cart as soon as you enter the store. Trust me when I say it hurts to hold clothes on one side of your arm for an extended amount of time while looking at other goodies. If you must have your handbag instead of a wristlet, look for a cart with a "seat belt" that works so that you can buckle your bag for safety and shop freely. *Here's a quick warning*, some stores do not have carts because either they are all gone, or the store uses baskets instead. When this is the case, grab what you can and ask the associate if you can put some items behind the counter while you are still browsing. Be sure to give the associate your name so that your items do not get nabbed. Speaking of nabbed, stay with your cart at all times! Guard it with your life! I have had people, including me, go through an abandoned cart thinking the items were available.

Lastly, if you plan to thrift for shoes, bring or wear footies/socks with you. Remember, the goal is to shop without restriction so that you can be free to navigate and get some great pieces!

BONUS! Find out your store's shipment day. Some stores receive shipments from retail stores and places those items in the "New Clothing" section or they mix them in with the other donations. Regardless, ask an employee, and they will tell you the best day to come for new items!

Speaking of donations, please consider donating items you no longer want to thrift stores in your area. My preference is Salvation Army as they have a pickup service. You can also partner with local shelters and thrift stores who are linked to charities and nonprofits!

Adrienne S. Young

Where to Thrift

Yes, there are certain areas where you'll want to thrift more than others. I map out where the more affluent neighborhoods are and find the closest stores in that area (check out Ayana of Thrifting Divas interview for a killer tip on this subject). I use this method the most when I'm out of town and want to thrift. Once, while I was waiting to pick up a large leather mirror I purchased for $20 (retailed at $199), I saw a gentleman drop off a hoverboard still in the box and a red bike that looked barely used. This particular Goodwill also had several Michael Kors bags (my friend Roshanda scored one), brand new Tahari boots, and a fur coat. Zip codes are your besties when it comes to finding stores that may carry name brand and newer items. Also, some cities offer thrift guides (Cape Cod does!) that will give you all the details about each store and what items they sell. If you do not want to go in the store, you can shop online! Here is a list from Instagram:

- @kthriftique
- @thriftontheave
- @yezterdaz
- @thegift_ofthrift
- @thredup
- @poshmark
- @currentboutique

Look for Quality Items

I have a personal rule for thrift store shopping that has saved me time and money: buy items that are made of quality material. Quality is key when thrifting. Even if the item is only one dollar, you do not want to waste it on something that may not last through one washing. As you select your items, put each one through a *quality inspection process*.

Look for malfunctions:

- Is the heel of the shoe scratched or is the heel itself worn down? Do not discount them as you can have them repaired (see care for your items section for shoes).
- Is there an obvious stain that cannot be removed?
- Are all the buttons there? Are any hanging on by a thread? Button everything to be sure.
- Is the zipper working properly? Zip it up and down a few times to test it.
- Are there any tears or holes? If yes, it's a no for me, as I don't have time to repair it. But, if you can repair it, by all means get it.

If the item passes my inspection process, it finds a home in my closet.

BONUS: Want to know if a garment is *new?* Of

course, if the clothing has the original tag on it, it's probably new. In addition, you can *check the label inside.* If the tag is flat and looks bright (like the J. Crew below) – more than likely it is new. If the tag has flipped up, looks wrinkly, or the letters on it have worn off, it has probably been worn a few times (like the BCBG).

Don't Go *Thrifting* Without Me!

Thrifting Interview
Ayana Pitterson | Thrifting Divas

Thrift • Fashion • Stylist

It's a way of life for me, then add fashion to it, and it's an added bonus.

What or who inspired you to join the world of thrifting?

I started thrifting back when I was a teenager in New York City. That's where I grew up and mostly not out of inspiration, but out of necessity. I'm the oldest of six and my mother just didn't have the funds to put us into the newest or the trendiest things. So, I started thrifting, and there was a cute little boy, an ex-boyfriend, with a store located right near his apartment. I stopped in there once, and from that one stop, I was pretty much hooked. At that point, I didn't see it as a making a statement or style statement. I just found cute things that I liked at prices I could afford, so I bought them. I didn't really think about it as an inspiration to others or anything at that time. It was a necessity.

What advice would you give to first-time thrifters?

I think determining your style before trying to go thrifting is really important. If you don't know what your style is, then going to a thrift store is going to become even more overwhelming. If you already know what your style is, but need to save money while buying great things, try to go with someone who already thrifts. That would be important because I don't want you to become so overwhelmed that you turn around and leave the store. I've even walked into thrift stores and come out overwhelmed. So, I would say go with someone first, who knows the lay of the land. They don't have to be an expert, but *definitely* go with someone who already thrifts.

Then the second thing is understanding how to set your expectations. A thrift store is not a retail store. If you are looking, try to start off slowly and build up. Maybe look at going to a consignment store. That is the first place I will take someone who's just not really sure about it. For the most part, consignment stores are going to be very organized, really nice and almost chic. It will remind you of going into a boutique. And once you see the prices, then you will know that, hey, if I went to the mall, this same J. Crew skirt would have been $68.

What are the one or two thrift finds that sent you into bliss?

I went by a consignment shop and I said, "Oh, I'm not even in the mood for them today. I'm just going to peek in only in the shoe section." I wasn't going to buy anything. I walked in and there's these boots and as soon as I picked one up I was like, "Wow, this feels amazing!" The boot had a heavy feeling to it. They were suede boots with fur cuffs around them. So, I knew right away it was real suede, but I had never heard of the designer.

It was called Aqua Talia. I didn't even care what the name was, I was going to get the boots! They were $25. I went home, looked up the designer, and the price was $650! I just started laughing. I was like, "You've got to be kidding me. Wait, what?" I looked into the brand and it's a very well-made brand. It's a weatherproof boot as well.

What will you never thrift?

Underwear. I'm not doing the underwear. I think underwear is cheap enough that I don't really need to thrift underwear. I know Victoria's Secret will have a sale every now and then, but everyone has sales on underwear.

What do you always thrift?

I always thrift sequence, all my fur coats are thrifted, and all my high-end designer pieces have always been thrifted.

How has your thrifting enhanced someone else's life?

About a year and a half ago when I wanted to really try my hand at styling, I offered a free styling session with me. Women had to write in as to why they thought they deserved this package. The package was three hours of me at their house going through their closet and giving style option. Then we would spend another three hours at thrift stores. I had over 60 women write in, and it was really touching. The stories they told were the things that I sometimes really, truly take for granted.

A lot of these women explained that based on so many different things that have happened in their lives, fashion had become something that was a true fear of theirs. Yet, they realized that they needed to do something about it. The woman that I picked to give the gift of restyling and thrifting to, her story was that she had been going through a major divorce and her self-esteem had been completely leveled out.

When you see this woman, she's gorgeous. So you will not think walking down the street that she has a self-esteem issue, which is always goes to show that what we show on the outside is not what's happening on the inside. Sometimes we have to slow down and realize that people have so many stories, and you can't judge a book by its cover. We went through the closet, we went through discussing all the things that were going on in her life and what she was doing with regards to fashion and was stopping her from feeling confident. We discussed the mental side of it all. Then we talked about the role clothes play in rebuilding confidence.

We overhauled the closet and built it back with things that really fit her, things that made her feel confident again, and items that would give her the confidence to know that she can do this on her own. She would no longer need someone like me telling her this goes with this, and that goes with that. She would be able to identify how to maximize the items in her closet. She wouldn't always have to rebuild by buying everything. There are a lot of pieces in everyone's closet that can be used, and she just didn't realize that. She needed to be shown how to use those things to her benefit.

Share a thrifting secret.

A thrifting secret I would give is how to find good thrift shops. People from different states often ask how to find the thrift shops in their area because the ones they go to don't seem to be the good ones. I would say go on the Internet and search for Zillow or download the Zillow app. Look in the area that has higher home prices. Notate the zip codes those homes are located in. You can even jot down the exact addresses of the homes. Next, go to Google maps and search for thrift stores near the homes or in the zip codes you notated.

What are your favorite thrift stores and why?

Goodwill has been my go-to store. On my way there, I'm always thrilled. I can find whatever I need at a goodwill. Goodwill to me is the mall.

Don't Go *Thrifting* Without Me!

How can we connect with you?

Thrifting Diva

THRIFT. FASHION. STYLIST.

Facebook: Thrifting Diva

Instagram: @thriftingdiva

Blog: www.thriftingdiva.com

Purchasing Unique Items

With uniqueness, I do not mean the pink flamingo dress and the matching blazer. Uniqueness is more so items that draw attention to you in a good way and spark a conversation. This item is not usually found in the mall and looks one of a kind. It could be a fur collar sweater or a hot pink leather skirt. Each time you wear this item, you expect compliments to pour in.

Before you purchase a unique item, ask yourself:

- Would I buy this item if it was full price?
- Do I have something I own that would go perfectly with this look?
- Can I wear this item and remix it with other items for a different look?

If the answer is yes, get it. If no, wheel it around the store to see if the desire is still there for purchase. If it is not, hang it back up for the one who is praying that you will.

Some of the best unique items are accessories. From the pop of color clutches to skinny belts, dangle earrings to stunning brooches, and classic sandals to peep toe heels, unique accessories can turn the simplest t-shirt and skirt into an eye-catching ensemble. Be sure to inspect these items for any malfunctions as well.

With earrings, make sure all the gems are in place and the earring "stick" is sturdy. With brooches, make sure they close all the way, and for a necklace, be sure it is not missing a clasp (although that is an easy fix). Later on, I will share with you how to properly clean these items prior to wearing them.

Bring a Thrifting Partner!

When I asked my thrift sisters their number one advice for first-time thrifters, they all said, "Shop with a person who has thrifted before!" I couldn't agree more. Shopping with a friend is helpful for three reasons:

1) Thrifting can be overwhelming, and a thrift buddy can help ease any anxiety and show you the ropes. i.e. how the store is laid out, where the dressing room is, etc.

2) It is fun to thrift with a friend who will say "yay" to the lace peplum top and "nay" to the polka dot trouser that does not flatter you.

3) Your thrift partner can help you find great items that she KNOWS you will rock!

Be Patient

If you want the bargains, you will have to hunt for them. Sometimes they won't jump out at you. You have to go get it! If you are short on time, I would not suggest you go to the thrift store for a specific item. There are **so** many choices, and you will either be frustrated looking or late for your next appointment.

When shopping for clothes, I highly recommend going through the section one item at a time. I know it is time-consuming, however, because of the many options, some clothes get "stuck" or "hidden" behind one another. I cannot tell you how many times I have found a brand-new shirt that was stuck behind the not so cute flowered one.

Also, exercise patience for the dressing room. You may have to wait to get in the dressing room to try on your selections (this is a good time to weed out the items you were debating on). If you have many things to try on, it will take some time to change in and out of items. My rule of thumb is to try on groups of items. For instance, I try on dresses first, then bottoms and tops together to see it as one complete outfit.

Adrienne S. Young

Thrifting Interview Questions

Keri Crutchfield | AdornedDc

Full-time Style Strategist: 6 years

Stylepreneur: 18 years

"Some women brag about how expensive their clothes are, I brag about how cheap mine was. Oh you like this? I thrifted it for $5.00"

What or who inspired you to join the world of thrifting?

My mom and grandmother have been thrifting for years. As early as I can remember, my mom would get up on Saturday mornings and take us (my two sisters and I) to thrift stores in Cambridge, MD. Buying everything from clothes to household collectibles. I learned there to carefully curate looks and meticulously pick out what was as close to "in" then as I could. At the time I was eight or nine years old and embarrassed to be shopping hand me downs. But as I grew so did my love for thrifting, second hand shopping, and finding unique pieces none of my friends would have from shopping mannequins at the mall. It became an art.

I soon realized I could find the same looks, if not better from whatever was in style and/or in season. So, I never stopped shopping there. Fast forward 20 years or so later. I still shop and style clients from second hand, recycled fashion. I don't follow trends much anymore when deciding my direction. I just go with what feels right. Pieces I will never see again and what makes a statement without making a sound.

Advice for 1ST Time Thrifter:

1. Go in with an open mind. There are so many misconceptions about thrifting. But an open mind is like an open portal, ready to receive! Ha! (no for real) If you go in thinking I am going to find some great pieces, or even a specific item. I guarantee you, you will.

2. Don't just shop your section/size- I shop all over the thrift store. Men's section, kids and even in the household section. I've been

known to make curtains…high fashion fabrics for killer looks that someone else would have walked by!!!! Know that your possibilities are endless.

Best Thrifted Item:

My first luxury find was a Fendi 2 pc jacket and pant suit. It was five sizes too big but nothing a sewing machine couldn't fix!!! I still have it. I got it from a bag sale. A bag sale allows you to put all you can in a brown bag for $4.00. It's over 25 years old and it still kills every time I wear it. It retails now for over $1100 and to think I folded it down in a brown bag for four bucks!!!

Since then I've snagged so many designer items. But another find that made my heart flutter was an ice blue 2 piece knit dress set, I found for $5.00. I liken it to a St. John knit but I don't think it has a tag inside. My husband LOVES it and the reaction I get from him whenever I put it on lets me know waaaay before we met GOD KNEW! I'd found it at least two years before meeting him and still wear it to this day.

P.S. ...it still has the same effect!

What will you never thrift?

I will probably never thrift underwear. Like panties! I think for safety precaution, it is the one thing that's completely off limits for me

What do you always thrift?

However, I do thrift lingerie, 50's dressing gowns and long DIOR, Oscar de la Renta nightgowns with trains that sweep across the levels of my home like no other. I use robes as caftans and some silk night shirts as killer day tops.

There is always something in the lingerie section that speaks to me. Soft, delicate, all things woman. I love them, even if it's a cami or night top used under a men's blazer to soften a look!

How has your thrifting enhanced someone else's life?

I look at it as my gifting… my marketplace ministry. It has become an altar of deliverance. I have prayed for several women, led women to Christ and been able to witness from a thrift day that was ordained by God. I've helped women feel better about themselves, think outside their comfort zone, and put together runway looks they would have never imaged from everyday pieces.

I have helped women find their voices and the power to tell their stories through carefully curated thrifted clothing. Clothes have history, they have endured…traveled time and speak to and for the woman wearing them! I use thrifting to help countless women manage their household (finances) by creating a monthly budget to shop from that saves them tons of money.

Share a thrifting secret.

Always wear a bodysuit, tights and fitted tee. Something you can put clothes over. It helps if there is no dressing room or you don't want to put clothing directly on your skin. You can make wherever you stand a changing station and if there are any irritants on the clothing, you are protected.

What are your favorite thrift stores and why?

Don't Go *Thrifting* Without Me!

My favorite thrift store is home on the Eastern Shore. It's called the Robin Hood shop. They have a monthly bag sale!!!! All you can fold down in a bag for $5.00. Also, because even where there isn't a bag sale, their prices are always so low, I just know I can get the most for my bucks.

How can we connect with you?

Tuesdays- I do **#thriftyTuesdays** on Instagram live, my stories where I offer pop up styling/shopping services. I show racks of plus size items, put looks together, and show tons of designer items found thrifting.

Follow me on Instagram: @adornedDC

Adrienne S. Young

To follow a day in the life my style files, search the following hashtags:

- ➢ #whereFAITHandFASHIONcollide
- ➢ #theMinistryofFASHION
- ➢ #discernmentofSTYLE

To shop items from my personal collection of thrifted, vintage items, follow: @shopmyclosetadc

Email: adornedDC@gmail.com for Consultations, to become a monthly client and have the thrift store sent to your door!

Pintrest: AdornedDc the lens of AdornedDC

Website/blog: www.adornedDC.com.

"Fashion for me has become a platform of change!"

Dressing Room 101

Some thrift stores do not have a dressing room. No worries, because you already have the solution to that problem with your thrifting uniform! If the dressing room is full, or if a store does not have dressing rooms, find an inconspicuous place in the store near a mirror where you can try on items.

If you enter a dressing room full of clothes, rejoice! That means someone has taken the time to grab some great pieces and discarded them just for you. I have found great items just by going through the dressing room pile. In addition, if the associates have started placing items back on the rack by the dressing room for restocking, it is even better! You can go through the rack, and if you find an item you like, you just removed one less thing for the associate to do.

Take the items you want and be kind to place items you do not want on the designated rack.

It is Time to Check Out!

You have gone through every rack. You tried on every piece. You put back what did not work, and now it's time to check out. Prior to getting in line, or if there is a line, here is how you can save time checking out:

- If price tags are used at this thrift store, make sure they are on the item. Some stores will not sell an item without one.
- Remove the hangers from your items and take the extra step of hanging them on the rack for the cashier if you can get to it.
- Fold the clothing to where the tag is visible if available; otherwise, have clothes or household items grouped together by type to be rung up together.
- Greet the cashier by name and ask him or her how their day is going. This extra step has less to do with speed and more about being a kind human. I will admit there have been times when I got an extra 10% off, favor is what we call it in the Christian community, just by striking up a conversation with the cashier. It pays to be nice!
- Have your method of payment ready. Cash is preferred as it keeps you under budget and is

great for the times with the debit/credit card machines are down.

- Thank the cashier, take your receipt (just in case you need to exchange an item) and grab your goodies, and sashay away (that is for the women).

BONUS: Some stores offer reward programs. Be sure to sign up for them if you frequent a store. Others give students and senior citizens a discount. I go with my mom on Tuesdays for that very reason...don't judge me. Always ask to see if there are even more ways you can save.

DOUBLE BONUS: Thrifting children's clothes is a must! For boys, sometimes it is hard to find items, but for girls (I have five nieces), I always rack up. Some of the best deals are found in children's consignment shops. Do a Google search for shops in your area and ask about how you can consign to make money as well!

Adrienne S. Young

Thrifting Interview

Samantha "Sammy" Davis | Thrift Babes

Dreamer • Doer • Believer in the power of you!

"I believe from the bottom of my heart that fashion can be a driving force for anyone on this planet to become the better version of themselves, pursue their goals, to find meaning in suffering, whatever it is that you're going through."

What or who led you to join the world of thrifting?

I've always been a thrifter. But I've always been a community builder. I've always been passionate about bringing people together. I only judge based on character and even then, I just believe it's about connecting with someone to bring out the higher version of themselves and sometimes humans just need love. I fell in love with fashion at a young age and did not have a huge piggy bank behind me. I discovered thrifting and I was blessed to go to school in a more urban environment.

When I moved to New York City to pursue fashion publishing, I discovered that wasn't the path for me. I decided that I actually couldn't connect with as many people as I felt my spirit was telling me that I could connect with. I thought it was supposed to be through publishing that I would empower women. Fast forward to now. I've been blogging, I've been selling, and I've been styling. I've run a vintage store for two years now. I also have thrift tours in New York City!.

Advice for a 1st time thrifter:

My number one piece of feedback is, if you can, go with an experienced thrifter. Now, I know that's not always possible, but look at it this way. You want to go to some sort of event and it's not in your comfort zone, but your friend invites you go. You're so much more likely to go with your friends who will be there. So, it's sort of the same thing, right? I mean we're all adults. We all should have 100% confidence, but I understand it can be kind of awkward walking into the store that you don't even know, so you feel like everyone's looking at you when in reality they aren't. If you go with an experienced thrifter, just allow them to walk you through garments and allow them to also dress you so that you just start to feel more comfortable.

Best thrifted item:

Girl, they are all my fave!! The first is a black hat that was $2 from Goodwill. When I put it on, it made me feel like I was in a Beyoncé music video and say, "I am hot in this hat!"

Currently, it's this bright pink fanny pack I found for $1, a pair of Levi's acid wash vintage denim jeans for $5.99, and my 90's Jordache jacket for $10!

What will you never thrift?

It used to be workout clothes, but now it's reversed. I will not buy second hand stuffed animals, very risky. Lice, bedbugs, which I have had in New York City. So, my advice to any parents is, even though it seems really appealing, please don't buy your child's stuffed animal from the thrift store. Um, what else? Yeah, definitely underwear, but it's not really sold except for lingerie, which I have purchased a few lingerie pieces but they're the baby doll and cami pieces. No furniture for me because I live in a 700 sq. ft. apartment, and I am not a DIYer!

What do you always thrift?

I always thrift my coats. I always thrift my dresses. I always thrift a t shirt. Eighty percent of my wardrobe is thrifted.

How have you enhanced someone else's life through thrifting?

It's just really about inspiring women to live their best life in a look for less. I believe from the bottom of my heart that fashion can be a driving force for anyone on this planet to become the better version of themselves, pursue their goals, to find meaning in suffering, and whatever it is that you're going through. I really, really, really believe that God gave us the ability to dress ourselves so that we could feel better and we can do better. That's really my intention behind the group, but it's wonderful because people share and connect with each other and it's growing even more international by the day.

Share a thrifting secret.

Wear something comfortable, like a catsuit or a fitted tee and leggings just in case there aren't any dressing rooms. Another secret is kind of terrible of me to share, but it's a secret. Don't tell anyone. Not all Salvation Army's do this, but we have found in New York City that sometimes things are very overpriced. I mean most of the time they're not. So, I don't want to discourage you from thriftng in New York City. Sometimes, I'm like "wow! I can't believe this is $8. It should be like $3!" In the past, because I bring so much business to the store, I saw a dress, and it was $20 dollars. I took the tag off and asked them to price it. They price it lower at $13. So, you know what, it's okay.

What are your favorite thrift stores and why?

I like Etsy, NYC Bargain thrift, Salvation Army on 46th Street, Astoria, and the Goodwill Outlet where you pay by the pound in Long Island.

Don't Go *Thrifting* Without Me!

How can we connect with you?

Instagram: @sammydtv

Facebook: www.facebook.com/groups/thriftbabes

My Air B&B experience NYC thrift store tour:
https://abnb.me/T4nvCZeZmR

Cleaning and Caring for Your Purchases

Your shopping trip was a success, and you are ready to rock your "new" blazer with the cute clutch, but first, you have to clean it. If the item is brand new, you may be okay to skip this step, but you still may want to invest a little time in making sure it is ready to go when you are ready to wear it.

Handbags

Items need:

- cleaning gloves
- vacuum (optional)
- Damp cloth (microfiber) or disinfectant wipe
- trash can

Grab the cleaning gloves, put them on, and shake out any debris into the trash can. Use the wand attachment of the vacuum cleaner to suck up any crumbs, lint, little bits of paper or other debris from the bottom of the purse. Unzip the zippers, and remove anything there (if you find money, rejoice!). Use a disinfectant wipe or a microfiber cloth with soap and water to clean up little marks on the purse lining and the outside. For outside marks, try fingernail polish remover with a cotton swab but be very careful and use it in a small area first so that you don't ruin the handbag.

If the purse is leather or faux leather, make it shine by rubbing it with a banana peel or mix vinegar with oil and use the microfiber cloth in circular motions to "wax it." The vinegar gently cleans the leather, and the olive oil breaks up dirt and stains while conditioning it. This same method can be used for furniture. Freshen the handbag by placing a dryer sheet inside.

Jewelry

Use rubbing alcohol or disinfectant wipe to clean the back of the earring. Be careful with fake jewels or painted jewelry as the rubbing alcohol could leak out and damage the finish. To prevent this damage, dip a cotton swab in water and add a drop of dish soap to clean it. I would suggest you discard the backs of earrings and use the ones you have. For clip-on earrings, the same method works. Air dry all jewelry.

Shoes

If you see black "skid" marks on a shoe, grab some nail polish remover and a cotton swab or pad. Test the area first to make sure it does not damage the material. Once you see how much pressure you need to apply and it will not damage the shoe, clean all the marks. Then, clean the shoe with a disinfectant wipe (testing the area), or soap and water inside the insole and on the outside. If you want extra cleaning power, spray the inside of the shoe with a disinfectant spray and let it air dry. For sneakers, you can wash them in your washer and air dry them. If the soles or heels are worn down, take this advice from Ayana of Thrifting Divas.

"Girl, get you a cobbler!!!!!! Not the pie, but a person who specializes in repairing shoes. At the end of the winter season, I take all of my leather boots to the cobbler and have them retap the soles and polish the leather for me. After trudging through the snow, and nasty winter, the boots can take a licking. However, after a trip to the cobbler, you are not going to believe how brand new your boots can look for the new season. This saves me tons of money in not having to buy certain boots over and over, while still giving them that pristine look."

Clothing

Check the labels to see how to properly launder the items. I wash most of my items on permanent press or gentle depending on the tag. Dry clean items can also be washed on this same setting, but dry clean **only** should be taken to a professional dry cleaner. Hang or lay flat to dry to prevent shrinkage, color loss and longer wear of your items. This care tip can be used on all your items, both thrifted and non-thrifted.

Don't Go *Thrifting* Without Me!

Thrifting Interview

Nina Clark | House of ANIN

THE EMPOWERING STYLIST

"We can go into a store and come out looking again, like a million bucks."

What or who inspired you to join the world of thrifting?

I would say my mother. Growing up, Saturdays was our mother daughter time, and would go to the thrift stores to shop. My mom has a natural gift to make something less costly look like a million bucks. 'Til this day, we still go thrifting together. So I would say definitely it will be my mom.

Adrienne S. Young

What advice would give to first-time thrifters?

My advice would be to make sure that you have plenty of time to look. Don't go if you're in a hurry or are short on time. And also, I would advise them to go comfortably that way you have time to look and you're comfortable while doing it.

What are the one or two thrift finds that sent you into bliss?

Mine was my Tory Burch boots. Oh my gosh, I absolutely love them! I paid $12 for them and they cost around $500.

What will you never thrift?

I would never thrift underwear. That's where I draw the line.

What do you always thrift?

Everything except the answered above. I practically thrift everything even for my household.

How has your thrifting enhanced someone else's life?

I think my thrifting has enhanced someone else's life by letting them know that it's part of my ministry; it's fulfilling your purpose and looking good doing it. You don't have to make an excuse of not being able to look the part because when you can go thrifting, and you can find what you need to look the way that you need to look. I have to say that even thrifting will enhance women's lives to be what they are called to be and not be held back by "I can't buy this or that," or by lack of finances. There is no excuse.

Share a thrifting secret.

Find high end stores near really nice neighborhoods because sometimes that can determine the different pieces that you will get in a thrift store is especially higher end things.

What are your favorite and/or go to thrift stores and why?

I really absolutely don't have a favorite. I just love a thrift store. I can be driving and I will see a thrift store and I will literally make a u turn. So I really don't have a favorite thrift store. I just enjoyed thrifting. I love making, um, I love making something new again.

How can we connect with you?

Facebook: Nina T. Clark

Instagram: @ninatclark

www.ninatuckerclark.com
houseofninaanin@gmail.com

Don't Go *Thrifting* Without Me!

Thrifting Interview

Wendy Derilus-Joseph | Dressing for Me & 365 Dresses

Vintage Thrifter • Lawyer • Style Blogger

A lover of anything empowering women, classic style, fashion, Diana Ross fanatic, thrifting, vintage, and maintaining a healthy lifestyle on a plant-based diet (vegan).

What or who inspired you to join the world of thrifting?

My mother introduced me to thrifting. When I was a little girl, I watched my mom pick up the neighborhood newspaper, search for garage sales throughout Brooklyn, and circle the ones she and her sister would visit on Saturday mornings. This was their Saturday morning routine.

What advice would you give to first-time thrifters?

Be patient and think outside the box. I never go into a thrift store with my mind set on a particular item. I think that's a set up for disappointment. Enter with an open mind.

What are the one or two thrift finds that sent you into bliss?

I have several thrift bliss moments. I've scored a Ted Baker skirt brand new with tag retail price $150.00 for $5.99. My second a Donna Karan sequin romper retail $350.00 for $18.00 while thrifting at a Goodwill in New York.

What will you never thrift?

I can't see myself thrifting sneakers and workout clothes. Perhaps, if they are new with tag but I cannot see myself wearing someone else's sweaty workout clothes.

What do you always thrift?

That's an easy one. DRESSES!!!!!!! I just adore dresses. It is one of the reasons I have my Facebook Group 365Dresses. When I walk into a thrift store, I go to the dress section first. I thrift dresses in both modern and vintage. Dresses are much easier to style, especially for a fashionista on the go like myself.

How has your thrifting enhanced someone else's life?

When I first started thrifting, no one really shared that information. Now that I share my thrifting experiences, finds, and fashion through my blog, people share with me that they've started thrifting and they find joy in it.

Share a thrifting secret.

Location matters. The nicer the neighborhood, the nicer the thrift store. While you can find gems in any second-hand store, from my experience, stores in wealthier areas often have higher end items.

What are your favorite go to thrift stores and why?

1. Goodwill - I travel often and when I do, a Goodwill is always easy to find, I'm familiar with Goodwill, and it will be less likely for me to be disappointed.

2. Poshmark - I can thrift shop from my bed. Nothing like a good online thrift shopping.

How can we connect with you?

Facebook: Wendy Joseph
Instagram: @JustJewels4U.
Blog: www.DressingForMe.com

Thrifting Housewares

Thrifting items for my home has been rewarding as I find unique pieces, or Target closeouts that fit my traditional style. I scored a $199 Pier One Snakeskin Mirror for $24.99 at Goodwill! Many of my pictures, decor pieces, pillows, curtains and bedding have been thrifted. You can find curtain rods, knobs for cabinets, blinds, pictures, lamps, vases, and the list goes on. If you need items for a specific project home project, look for Habitat for Humanity Restores. When thrifting home items, here is what you need to know.

Furniture

Even if you want a piece of furniture just for decoration and not for the purpose it is intended, inspect it carefully. If you plan to actually use chairs and couches, here are some suggestions:

- Sit on them to see if they feel as good as they look.
- Look for holes and stains by walking all around it.
- Take the cushions out to check the quality of the springs.
- Inspect the legs for stability and look for screws that may need tightening or need to be replaced.

Don't discount a piece of furniture because it does not look good to you. Just like beauty is only skin deep, so can a bookshelf be with a little TLC. You can do a DIY and strip the wood and repaint it to fit your style. In Ayana's Thrifting Divas group, one of the members, Precious Haney-Adams, repurposed these beautiful chairs.

Books, CDs and DVDs

Some of my best reads for me and my sons have come from the thrift store. You can get novel series, how-to books, cookbooks, and more for less than $1. Some stores section the books by genre and type (hardback or paperback) making it easier to see what you may have in mind. With CDs and DVDs, open the cases to check that the correct disc is in it and look for scratches. You can also find great board games but be cautious as some of the pieces may be missing.

Bedding and Curtains

Most stores have their bedding in a section on hangers. Inspect it carefully. You may have to examine it closely to see what size it is as most comforters do not have the size labeled (most are on the bag it came in). At Goodwill, there are baskets on top of the clothing racks that house brand new unopened curtains and sheer panels. Once, I bought a Martha Stewart set with the bedding, pillows, and bed skirt for $25 when it retailed $150! For care, launder it as the label says.

Holiday & Event Thrifting

Did you know thrift stores carry décor items just for the holidays? I thrifted a pre-lit Christmas tree, retailed $199.99 for $39.99! You may see items such as wrapping paper, ornaments, tree lights, tableware, wreaths, signs, and the list goes on! For events, there are many wedding items, plate chargers, stemware, linens, candles and more that can be used to decorate. My mom thrifted a wedding dress (you can save so much money and thrift a wedding dress by the way) and used the train as a tablecloth for my vendor event! The possibilities are endless.

BONUS: When purchasing furniture items from Goodwill, there will be a perforated price tag on it. You take the bottom one to the register, pay for it, go back to the item to place a red sold sign on it, and then drive around back to pick it up. If you are 100% sure you want the item, do not hesitate to take the tag before someone else gets it. For lamps, pre-lit Christmas trees, Christmas lights, and electric items, ask the associate if you can plug them in to make sure they work.

Thrifting Interview

Teresa B. Niles | Restyled by Niles

What or who led you to join the world of thrifting?

Initially, I was introduced to thrifting by mom. My mom had three kids. As a single parent, she thrifted basically because she had to. As a child that was very embarrassing. We did not want anyone to see us in the Salvation Army. So, we would duck. That went on until I was able to get a job. I had a child, and after graduating college, I was working for a nonprofit as an administrative assistant. I was told by one of the directors that a new position was coming open and I had the skills and qualifications, but they were concerned about my image. I needed to portray the look to go to regional meetings and represent the organization. Being a single parent that kind of alarmed me because I really didn't have the budget to buy the clothing and things that others had.

The Director speaking with me was also an attorney. She must have sensed my hesitation because she said, "I'm going to take you where I shop." I remember thinking, "Okay, really?" Because, seeing how she dressed, I knew I couldn't afford those things. But we ended up meeting one afternoon and she took me. I think God definitely has a sense of humor. She took me to the Salvation Army... back to the very place that I hated and didn't want to be seen in.

Nevertheless, we went there to shop, and she helped me pick some blazers, a few staple pieces, and other items. From there, I began to add those items with my little black dress and things that I already had and she gave me some pointers to basically upgrade my look. I was 23 or 24 years old and with her help, I began to change my look. It didn't take long for people to begin to notice. I ended up getting the promotion and I got a $7,000 raise! I was the office manager, and I supervised a couple of people, but it all came through thrifting and being able to build a wardrobe. I had a professional wardrobe on a budget that I could afford as a single parent.

What advice would you give to first-time thrifters?

My advice is, first of all, it can be overwhelming. So, pick what you want or a section. If you're looking for dresses, just shop that section and then try to shop the entire store. I know for some people that I've talked to, they ended up leaving with nothing because they're overwhelmed. Instead, go in with the vision of what you want. If you're looking for blazers, just shop that particular area and get your blazers. From there, build a vision of what you want your wardrobe to look like. I write what I'm looking for… what I want because if not, I ended up coming out with a lot of things I don't need.

Best Thrifted Item:

My favorite piece, I didn't find it. One of my friends in Atlanta found it for me. It was a St. John Suit for $1! I wore to the prom and then I wore it on a cruise and then I sold it. I sold it because I wore it three times. I think I have pictures of three different events in it. I took it to the consignment store and I think they sold it for like $300. So I made $150 off of it.

What will you never thrift?

Definitely, no undergarments and nothing that requires alterations. When I buy it, it's got to be ready to dry, clean, wash and be ready to wear.

What do you always thrift?

I always thrift dresses and shoes.

How has your thrifting enhanced someone else's life?

I've been able to share this gift with other women. I believe God has allowed it to be a platform for me. I've met so many women. I remember this young lady T. She was going through something with her husband and she just pretty much let herself go. I remember us thrifting and putting makeup on her. She went to a birthday party where her husband was in attendance, and he didn't even recognize her. He looked and had to take a second look! Ten dollars changed her whole look, her whole attitude, and her whole spirit.

Share a thrifting secret.

I like pussy-bow blouses, and when I'm looking at a rack, I scan the very top of them just to see if I see the neckline going up like that [into a bow].I can kind of eye it by going down the aisle before scanning the rack.

Favorite thrift stores and why?

Goodwill on Garners Ferry Road. I like this store because the merchandise is always awesome, and the customer service is amazing.

How can we connect with you?

Website: www.restyledbyniles.com
Facebook: www.facebook.com/restyledbyniles

Bonus Thrift Tips!

1. Have items in mind that you want to thrift. Consider creating a "***Thrift this Look***" Wishlist board on Pinterest so that you can pull it up on your smartphone while shopping.

2. Budget your time. Regardless if you are pressed for time or not, budget how long you will remain in a store to maximize the time there. I set a timer on my phone for 15-30 minutes so that I can stay focused on what I am looking for.

3. Kill two birds with one stone. Shop where there are two thrift stores nearby, especially if you are looking for a particular item and do not find it at one store.

4. Use the bathroom before you leave and pack snacks and water!

5. For my female thrifters, do not limit yourself to just the women's section. Shop in the junior, children or men section as some items for ladies end up there. Because some thrift stores do not separate the coat section by gender, be sure to go through those racks carefully.

6. Check your thrift store hours. Some smaller thrift stores are only open certain days of the

week for limited times. Be sure they are open the day you want to go!

7. Thrifting is a community. Do not be surprised if a perfect stranger asks if you like something or you may ask a perfect stranger a question. I have been blessed by conversations over the size of a comforter, and one person gave me the inside scoop of other nearby stores with great deals!

A THRIFT DAY AT A GLANCE

Let's summarize what a typical day of thrifting will look like for you.

- Map out which store(s) you will visit
- Put on your thrifting uniform and grab your wristlet
- Have your thrift wish list ready
- Eat and use the bathroom
- Pick up a friend or have them meet you there
- Say a prayer before you get out the car
- Set a timer if you are pressed for time
- Grab a cart
- Go to the section you have on your list
- Get your items, inspect them, try them on
- Head to the register
- Walk out with your finds rejoicing!

You may walk out and have nothing to show for your efforts. I went to four different thrift stores in one day and walked out empty handed. I chalked it up to "maybe this day is not the best day or the best time to thrift" because I have been in the same stores before and racked up. Disappointment in thrifting is real, but the great thing is, there is always tomorrow and there are other stores that may have exactly want you want.

Don't Go *Thrifting* Without Me!

Just make sure the next time you go, you do not go without me!

BONUS SECTION:
HOW TO Get an entire wardrobe for <u>FREE!</u>

In addition to thrifting, I LOVE hosting and attending swap parties with my *stylish* friends. Yes, I did say stylish. It is important to swap items with those who have a similar taste as yours so that you KNOW you will score some great pieces. Also, be sure to invite sisters of all shapes, and that includes shoe sizes. My friends and I swap EVERYTHING: housewares, books, accessories, clothes and shoes. We also bring food to the fellowship. Over the years, I bought clothing racks and separated the items by size and style. We laugh so much during this time as we try to "steal" items away from each other. Everyone always walks away with MORE than what they came with.

Swap parties or swap with a friend!

Gather friends and their excess stuff for this thrifty get-together and start trading.

Swap Party Basics

Why do it: Beyond being economical, eco-friendly, and an excuse to clean out your closet, a swap party with friends is far more fun than a yard sale with strangers.

Whom to invite: Friends with similar taste. For a good variety of merchandise, eight people is a manageable number, though anywhere from 3 to 20 is doable.

Invitation or e-mail? Send a free customizable Evite, Facebook invite, email invite, or by hand. Give guests two weeks' notice to start gathering their belongings.

Serve food! (themes around the season work great!)

Be clear about what's swap-worthy. Ask friends to bring clean goods that are new or in gently used condition. Provide guests with an extra tote bag for carting home their finds.

Stock up on supplies. Guests can claim desired items using clothes pins. Also, gather hangers and door knob hangers to separate clothes items.

Swap Party Success!

Establish a system. Choose one of the following swapping strategies, which should be explained in your Evite or at the start of the party.

Take turns shopping. Draw straws to pick who shops first. Limit the number of items to three per turn to keep it fair and moving fast.

- **Use tokens.** The host hands out a token for every item a guest donates. If a person brings

10 items, she gets 10 tokens with which she can purchase 10 new items.

- **Keep the numbers even.** Everybody goes home with the same number of items that they donated.
- **Tip:** Give guests room to spread out their items by clearing off surfaces, such as dining and side tables, and using bins and trunks to serve as display space.
- **For "ties."** Take the clips off the garment, place them in a bowl, and draw a winner!
- **Donate.** Donate items that are left over to local women shelters or a thrift store. You can schedule a pickup in advance!

Consign your clothes (from moneycrashers.com)

Consignment Stores typically work in two ways: upfront payments or profit sharing. There are pros and cons to each method, and not every consignment store offers both options.

When you're offered an upfront payment for your gear, a store employee will go through your offerings to see what would be able to be resold in the shop. Generally, there is a set price for each item, such as $10 for a pair of shoes or $5 for a shirt. Once all the items have been selected for consignment, the remainder can be taken home or donated to charity.

Then, the prices of all the clothes and goods are added up, and you're offered an amount in cash or in store credit on the spot.

Often, the store credit amount is higher because it entices you to keep the money in-house. But if your bank account is hungry, it might be a good idea to accept the cash. Keep in mind that you don't have to take the offer – if you feel that it's too low, you can respectfully decline and head somewhere else.

Shop in your own closet

Take out everything you own, and you may discover some pieces you forgot all about! Be inspired by a Pinterest board and begin forming outfits to mix and match. Take a picture of your "new" outfits and save them to your board for future reference.

Adrienne Young's mission is to love, live and lead on purpose, with purpose in every area of her life. As an avid thrifter, she built a community of over 2,000 women and inspired them with her thrifted looks, and when God asked her to give that community away to focus on full-time ministry, she obeyed. Some four years later, He allowed her to complete this book you're holding and share her passion for looking your best for less. Many say she is anointed to thrift and has an eagle eye for great pieces. May what you read in this book activate that same thrift grace in your life. May you find amazing pieces that make you giddy like a child on Christmas morning. May you experience thrifting in a way that enriches your life and adds no sorrow to it (Proverbs 10:22).

Adrienne Young is the Chief Visionary Warrior and Founder of Remnant Warriors Global, Inc., a nonprofit organization whose mission is for women to know how powerful they are and to walk in their Kingdom authority. She gets to touch the lives of over 7,000 women on a weekly in her Women Who War Facebook community via Bible studies and all throughout the year, they fellowship in prayer gatherings and gather once a year for the Warriors United Conference.

Adrienne takes her sixteen plus years of experience in education and John C. Maxwell certification to influence women of faith entrepreneurs and has been sought out by Fortune 500 companies for personal and professional development. Whether she is leading Bible studies, preaching the Word of God, giving captivating keynote speeches, or presenting practical ways to grow businesses and ministries, any encounter with Adrienne will push you into greatness to live your best life unto the Lord. Adrienne is married to Eddie, and they live in Fort Mill, SC with their two sons.